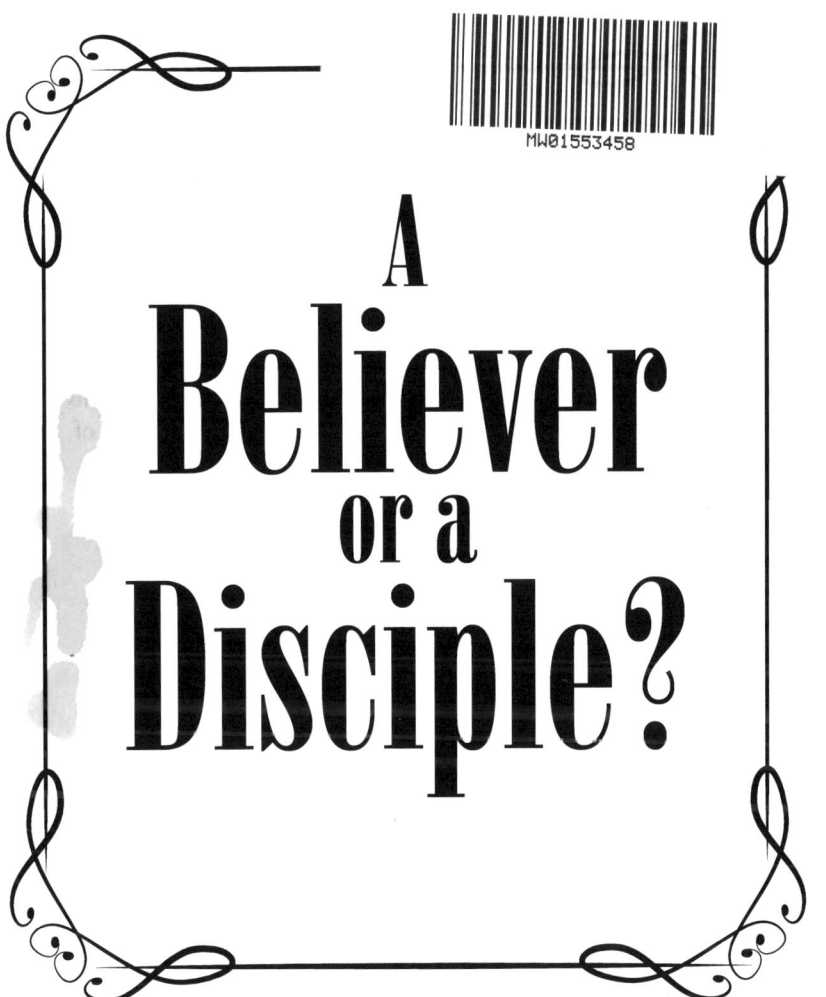

A Believer or a Disciple?

Andrew Wommack

© Copyright 2025 – Andrew Wommack

Printed in the United States of America. All rights reserved. No portion of this book may be reproduced, stored in a retrieval system, or transmitted in any form or by any means—electronic, mechanical, photocopy, recording, scanning, or other—except for brief quotations in critical reviews or articles, without the prior written permission of the publisher.

Unless otherwise indicated, all Scripture quotations are taken from the King James Version® of the Bible. Copyright © by the British Crown. Public domain.

Scripture quotations marked (NIV) are taken from the Holy Bible, New International Version®, NIV®. Copyright © 1973, 1978, 1984, 2011 by Biblica, Inc.™ Used by permission of Zondervan. All rights reserved worldwide. www.zondervan.com The "NIV" and "New International Version" are trademarks registered in the United States Patent and Trademark Office by Biblica, Inc.™

Published by Andrew Wommack Ministries, Inc.

Woodland Park, CO 80863

ISBN 13 TP: 978-1-59548-753-7

For Worldwide Distribution, Printed in the USA

1 2 3 4 5 6 / 28 27 26 25

Contents

What's the Difference? 1
Believers But Not Disciples 3
Evangelism *Plus* Discipleship 11
Discipleship Brings True Freedom 18
Appendix A 29
End Notes 31
Receive Jesus as Your Savior 33
Receive the Holy Spirit 35

Would you like to get more out of this teaching?

Scan the QR code to access this teaching in video or audio formats to help you dive even deeper as you study.

Accessing the teaching this way will help you get even more out of this booklet.

awmi.net/browse

What's the Difference?

This is a question many Christians have never asked. In fact, the terms "believer" and "disciple" are often used interchangeably. But there is a difference.

This can be seen very clearly in Jesus' own words from John 8:30-32:

> *As he spake these words, many believed on him. Then said Jesus to those Jews which believed on him, If ye continue in my word, then are ye my disciples indeed; And ye shall know the truth, and the truth shall make you free.*

Jesus' answer to the question, "Who are you?" in John 8:25 caused many of the people to believe on Him (John 8:30). Praise God! That's good, but Jesus went on to say to those who believed that they wouldn't be true disciples unless they continued in His Word.

Wow! This is amazing! This is something that is very rarely said in modern-day churches. *Jesus clearly made a distinction between being a believer and a disciple.* How many ministers have done that? If Jesus saw them as two distinct things, so should we.

Jesus said that if they would continue in His Word then they would become disciples *indeed*. The word indeed means in truth. It actually comes from compounding the two words, "in" and "deed," signifying something that was not only true in words but also factual in deeds or actions.[1]

The word disciple comes from the Greek word *mathetes* which means, "a learner, i.e. pupil."[2] *W.E. Vine's Expository Dictionary of New Testament Words* defines this Greek word as "indicating thought accompanied by endeavor… hence it denotes one who follows one's teaching…not only a pupil, but an adherent; hence they are spoken of as imitators of their teacher."[3]

This is describing a disciple as someone who has continued in their faith until their actions conform to their beliefs. This is like a person who has been an apprentice. They not only learn from teaching but put into practice what they've learned.

Or as Jesus put it, a disciple is a person who *continues* in His Word until they get set free. Anyone who is still bound isn't a disciple. This isn't saying they aren't saved, and it's not saying this freedom comes instantly. It's a process. But a true disciple is a person who has continued in the truth of God's Word until freedom is evident in their life.

I believe you can be saved and on your way to heaven but still be bound by poverty, sickness, and other challenges of this life. You don't have to be a disciple to go to heaven. In fact, you will probably get there quicker if you aren't a disciple, because you won't know how to walk in the health and victory that Jesus provided.

Believers But Not Disciples

If there are disciples *indeed*, then there are those who are not true disciples. They might be believers but not disciples.

We have billions of people on the planet today who claim to be Christians, but if they were arrested for being Christians, there wouldn't be enough evidence in their actions to convict them. Millions, possibly billions, are Christians in name only. They aren't true believers, and they certainly aren't disciples.

You can be a believer without being a disciple, but you can't be a disciple without being a believer.

The thief on the cross was a believer, but he wasn't a disciple. He could only claim to be a disciple in the sense that he acted on all he knew within the limited time and opportunity available to him, but he died within hours of making his request for Jesus to remember him (Luke 23:42). The thief didn't have time to continue in Jesus' words and grow into a disciple. Yet, Jesus said he would be with Him that day in Paradise.

From this example, we can clearly see that a person who truly believes and professes with his mouth that Jesus is the Christ is saved (Rom. 10:9). Therefore, *faith alone saves, but saving faith is never alone*. Something is seriously wrong with anyone who has the opportunity and understanding to become a disciple and yet chooses not to do so. Are they truly saved?

It's not always easy to tell if a person's faith is the true, saving type of faith. The thief on the cross simply asked Jesus to remember him when he came into His kingdom (Luke 23:42). He didn't join a church, get water baptized, take communion, read the Bible, or go through any of the religious rites associated with being saved. Yet Jesus promised him that he would be in paradise with Him that very day (Luke 23:43).

So, we see that salvation is as simple as "believe and receive or doubt and do without." We can't see a person's heart (1 Sam. 16:7); therefore, we can't tell if their faith is heartfelt by just looking at their outward appearance. But a disciple is a person who has continued following Jesus until they get set free (John 8:32). That makes it easy to tell if a person is a disciple, or in the process of becoming a disciple.

One of the great tragedies in the modern church is that we have forsaken Jesus' command to make disciples and have only been making converts. Jesus said in Matthew 28:19-20 (NIV),

Therefore go and make disciples of all nations, baptizing them in the name of the Father and of the Son and of the Holy Spirit, and teaching them to obey everything I have commanded you. And surely I am with you always, to the very end of the age.

Salvation is as simple as confessing with our mouths and believing in our hearts that Jesus is Lord (Rom.

10:9-10), but it's not that easy. We have to believe with all our hearts (Acts 8:37), which will result in actions. It's not our actions that produce faith, but true faith will produce actions. (James 2:18-20).

The thief on the cross got saved by calling on the name of the Lord (Rom. 10:13), but he died before he had the opportunity to continue learning and growing in his faith. Likewise, I'm sure there are people who have believed for their eternal salvation because that's all they've heard. Faith comes through hearing God's Word (Rom. 10:17). If they never hear about the claims the Lord has on our lives for discipleship, they won't have faith to pursue that.

James said,

Even so faith, if it hath not works, is dead, being alone.

James 2:17

True Bible faith will be expressed through actions, but it's not the actions that save. Faith in what Jesus did for us is the saving element (Rom. 3:28), not what we do for Him. But true faith has to be expressed through actions.

If we were together in a building and I told you the building was on fire and we would die if we didn't escape, you would do something if you really believed me. There is room for different actions. You could faint, scream, try to put the fire out, or run. But if you truly believed me, you would act. We would consider a person crazy who would just sit there and say, "I believe you," but did nothing. True faith demands action.

Romans 10:10 says we must believe from the heart and confess with our mouths in order to be saved. In other words, inner belief will be confirmed by outward actions. Those actions can be as simple as the thief's response to Jesus as he hung on the cross, but true faith has to be expressed, or it's dead (James 2:20).

Looking again at the great commission Jesus gave us in Matthew 28:19-20, we were commanded to make disciples, not converts. Somehow, the church changed this command about making disciples to just having people pray to receive salvation. Making disciples has not been the priority.

Many evangelists are so focused on getting people born again that they don't follow through after leading someone to pray and receive salvation. That's comparable to a person who loves babies so much that they do whatever is necessary to help the mother deliver a healthy child. But after the birth, they throw the baby aside and move on to see another baby born. Anyone who gives birth has a duty—actually, they have a responsibility—to make sure that the baby is taken care of so they can grow and mature.

It would be considered a criminal act for a doctor to deliver a baby and then throw it aside to go deliver another baby. As much as they might want to help deliver another baby, they have a responsibility to nurture the child they just delivered or entrust it to someone they've designated to care for newborns. The doctor must take steps to see that the baby has the opportunity to survive and thrive.

But many modern-day evangelists aren't concerned about bringing those they share the Gospel with into discipleship. It's all about getting them saved, and then they go looking for someone else to share the Gospel with. I have the same enthusiasm to see people saved, but Jesus' way of making disciples is better.

If a person had such an evangelistic zeal that they led one thousand people to the Lord every year for thirty-five years (the lifespan of a typical ministry), that would be exceptional. Most Christians don't lead anyone to the Lord in their lifetime. However, thirty-five thousand new believers still wouldn't make a dent in the spiritual well-being of some of our larger cities. Large numbers of believers already exist in these cities, yet their impact is minimal.

However, if the same person who had a passion to get people born again also did what the Lord commanded and made disciples of them, they would have a much greater impact in the long run. Consider this: If that person led just one person to the Lord every six months and then took them under their wing and discipled them, after six months there would be two disciples. Each of these disciples would then reach another person and disciple them.

That would produce four disciples by the end of the first year compared to one thousand believers by the evangelistic method. Each disciple, however, would keep reaching out, making another disciple every six months. This would double the number of disciples every six months, and at the end of just sixteen and a half years, there would be over 8.5 billion disciples, as shown in Appendix A. That's more than the current population of the world.

It's short-sighted to just get people to repeat a prayer so they can go to heaven. It's not what Jesus commanded us to do, and it produces people who claim to be Christians but can't demonstrate their faith through their lives. And worst of all, it gives many a false belief that they are right with God because they've repeated some words or filled out a card to join a church.

I'm sure all of us have heard someone criticize the hypocrites down at the church. That has turned multitudes away from the Lord. Unfortunately, many "believers" are negative witnesses for the Lord.

Mahatma Gandhi was exiled from India for years because of his political beliefs. While in Africa, he read the New Testament and was convinced that Jesus was the Christ. He went to a Presbyterian church to make a profession of his faith in Jesus, but they turned him away because of the color of his skin. He said, "I would have been a Christian if I hadn't met one."[4]

Those Presbyterian missionaries might have been believers. I suspect they were because they had moved to a foreign country to share the Gospel with people. But they weren't disciples. The Lord would never discriminate against a person because of the color of their skin. Immature believers have been the source of all kinds of mistreatment of others, turning countless numbers away from the Lord because of the way He is misrepresented.

Mahatma Gandhi went back to India and led 750 million Indians to independence from Great Britain. He could have influenced all of those people with Christianity, but a believer who was not a disciple turned him away from the Lord. What a pity. It could have been very different.

Evangelism *Plus* Discipleship

Don Krow was a very close friend and minister with me for decades. He had a zeal for leading people to the Lord and would often see someone born again daily. That was wonderful, but I asked him what happened to them after they prayed with him. In most cases, he didn't know. Our discussions about this led to us jointly producing a program we call *Discipleship Evangelism*. It is forty-eight lessons that take a person from the most basic truths of Christianity to being a mature disciple, equipping them to make other disciples. Millions of people worldwide have gone through it.

So, Don started approaching people about discipleship instead of just talking to them about the initial salvation experience. For example, he started taking food to apartments and asking if the people had any other needs, such as healing or financial problems.

I remember one instance where he took food to a couple who were just living together. They said they also needed healing since the man couldn't work because of his back problems. Instead of talking to them first about receiving salvation, Don started ministering to them where they were. He opened up the Bible and taught them about healing. He prayed with the man, and he was instantly healed. The couple was so shocked that they wanted to learn more, so they invited Don back the next week to share more with them. They were being discipled without knowing it.

After a few weeks of study, Don had the man read the scriptures about the prodigal son from Luke 15. When he got to the part where the son decided to return to his father, Don stopped the man and asked him how he thought the father would respond. The man responded the way he knew his own father would respond to him. He knew he would tell him there was no way he would take him back. He had made his bed, and he would have to lie in it.

So, Don had him continue reading about how the father received the prodigal son with open arms and even threw a party for him. The man Don was discipling stopped and said, "Are you telling me that the Lord would accept me after all the things I've done?" Don told him to read it again. He read it again and asked the same question. Don told him to read it again.

After the third time this man read the father's reaction to the prodigal son, he fell on his knees and called out to Jesus for forgiveness. He and his girlfriend both received the Lord right there in their apartment. They went on to be baptized in water. I was privileged to lead them into the baptism of the Holy Spirit, and they got plugged into a local church and began to grow in the Lord.

Someone might counter by saying, "Why would Don prioritize getting them healed, fixing their finances, or facilitating their marriage if they weren't born again yet?" I agree that receiving salvation is more important than any of those other things. But you can't truly disciple a person in any of those areas without inevitably bringing them to a decision about receiving forgiveness for their sins.

For example, if you were discipling a man about how to deal with his marriage problems, you would use Paul's instructions about husbands loving their wives as the Lord loves the church (Eph. 5:25). It's not natural to love others more than we love ourselves. It takes God's supernatural love to make marriage work. To continue the discipleship process, the man would have to repent and receive God's love for himself because he can't give away what he doesn't have.

Here's another example: If you were discipling someone in the area of finances, you would have to use scriptures that encourage giving. This is counterintuitive to our natural minds. After all, if what we have is not enough, how could giving some away improve our situation? To continue in the discipleship process, the person would have to open up to the truth of God's Word and receive the new birth; otherwise, they would never be able to operate in giving and receiving as the Bible teaches.

When getting sins forgiven is the goal, then once a person turns to the Lord and gets assurance they are forgiven, they've reached their objective. They've got their ticket to heaven and lost their incentive to seek the Lord further. That's the reason we see so many lukewarm "Christians." They were told salvation is all about getting their sins forgiven so they can go to heaven. They don't know about having a vibrant relationship with the Lord *now*, in this life. They are just saved and stuck, waiting on heaven.

That's not true in all cases. Many people are so thankful to be forgiven of their sins that they fall in love with the Lord and can't get enough of Him. As a result, they disciple themselves. That's pretty much what I did. If you live through that process, it makes a great testimony, but there is a better way. We need to be discipled by a mature disciple.

John 3:16 is perhaps the most well-known scripture in the Bible:

For God so loved the world, that he gave his only begotten Son, that whosoever believeth in him should not perish, but have everlasting life.

That scripture may be well known, but it's not well understood. Jesus wasn't saying that the purpose of salvation was getting our sins forgiven so we wouldn't perish. That's part of it. But Jesus went on to say it was so we could have everlasting life.

Everlasting life isn't just living forever. Everyone is going to do that. Even those who reject the salvation offered by Jesus will live forever. They will simply live forever in torment, separated from God and all that is good.

Someone might say, "Well, everlasting life is living forever in heaven instead of hell." But the Bible says we have everlasting life now, on this side of heaven (John 3:36; 4:14; John 5:24; John 6:27, 40, 47; and John 12:50).

Jesus, the Author of eternal life, defined it in John 17:3:

And this is life eternal, that they might know thee the only true God, and Jesus Christ, whom thou hast sent.

Eternal life is knowing God the Father and Jesus Christ. And this isn't describing just knowing about God and Jesus on an intellectual level. Genesis 4:1 says, "*And Adam knew Eve his wife; and she conceived, and bare Cain...*" Adam knowing Eve produced a child. The biblical word "know" describes an intimate, experiential knowledge.

It's true that Jesus gave Himself for our sins so that we wouldn't perish, but according to John 3:16, the real goal of salvation was so that we could have everlasting life—a close, intimate, personal relationship with the Lord. If all a person does is get their sins forgiven and a ticket to heaven, then they are missing the real purpose of salvation according to Jesus (John 3:16).

Sin was like a barrier that separated us from God. As Isaiah said,

Behold, the Lord's hand is not shortened, that it cannot save; neither his ear heavy, that it cannot

hear: But your iniquities have separated between you and your God, and your sins have hid his *face from you, that he will not hear.*

Isaiah 59:1-2

Sin barred us from an intimate relationship with the Lord. Jesus bore our sins and removed that barrier. But was it just so we could go to heaven? That's part of it. And if that's all there was to salvation, it would be much more than any of us deserve, and I would preach it to all who would listen. But Jesus removed the sin barrier so we could have intimate relationship with Him *now*, in this present life.

Because the church has been preaching "get saved so you can go to heaven," once people get assurance that their sins are forgiven and their ticket to heaven has been purchased, they just sit on their "blessed assurance," waiting on eternity. But it's not all about the "sweet by and by." We can have "steak on our plate while we wait." Heaven is going to be a blast, but Jesus came to give us abundant life on this side of heaven too (John 10:10).

My whole ministry is geared toward making disciples who experience everlasting life here and now and are able to share it with others. That's why I started producing teaching materials and traveling to hold conferences with a strong emphasis on teaching God's Word. I not only proclaim truth on my TV programs, but I explain truth with the goal of producing disciples. Our ultimate disciple-making machines are our Charis Bible Colleges scattered all over the world.

I get greater joy when I see my disciples produce fruit than when I am the one praying and getting results. It's only through making disciples that we are ever going to reach the world. Anyone who is not making disciples ultimately fails. We all have an expiration date, and unless we are raising up others who can do what we do, our ministry eventually comes to an end. But those who make disciples keep the truth of the Gospel going from generation to generation. That's the Bible method.

Discipleship Brings True Freedom

When Jesus told those who believed on Him that they must continue in His Word until they got set free, they were offended. That might be the reaction of someone reading this. You've been taught that just believing is enough, and you don't like someone telling you there is more. That's exactly how these people in John 8 reacted. They told Jesus they had never been in bondage to any man (John 8:33). How could He be telling them they needed to be made free?

This is amazing when you consider the fact that the whole Jewish nation was under the oppression of the Roman government. Surely, we've all seen the biblical movies about the hardships the Romans imposed on the conquered Jews of Jesus' day. They claimed to be free, but they weren't. They had lived with oppression so long that they didn't know they were oppressed.

Jesus went on to tell them that whoever commits sin is the slave of sin. Therefore, they were all slaves to sin and needed the freedom that only comes through faith in Jesus. "*If the Son therefore shall make you free, ye shall be free indeed*" (John 8:36). That sounds just like, "*If you continue in my word, then are ye my disciples indeed; and ye shall know the truth, and the truth shall make you free.*" (John 8:31-32).

Notice that it's only the truth *we know* that makes us free. What we don't know is killing us (Hos. 4:6).

These Jews had adjusted to their situation so much that they didn't even realize how bound they were. Likewise, many today have adjusted to their "less-than-God-provided" lives. They look around at others, and if they are doing as well as the average person, they think everything is okay. But the Lord died to deliver us from this present evil world (Gal. 1:4), not just the judgment to come. Jesus told us to pray for His will to be done on earth as it is in heaven (Matt. 6:10). Is your experience here on earth like it's going to be in heaven?

Most of us are living way below what Jesus purchased for us in this life. Continuing in His Word and becoming a disciple is the only way to be set free to experience the abundant life Jesus died to give us in this present life. One of the greatest things we can do for others is become a disciple so we can set others free. Only a free man can set someone else free.

These Jews were claiming a relationship with the Lord through Abraham. But that's not how it works. The Lord doesn't have any grandchildren. Everyone must have their own personal relationship with the Lord. No one can claim they are a believer because their parents were believers or because they associate with others who claim to be Christians. I actually had a man tell me he was a believer because he had a coin in his pocket that had "In God We Trust" engraved on it.

Jesus acknowledged that they were descendants of Abraham, but He told them they weren't true children of Abraham (John 8:37-38). That really incensed them. Jesus responded by saying if they were the true children of Abraham, they would have the faith of Abraham. Instead, He pointed out that they were trying to kill Him (John 8:40).

They persisted that they were the free children of Abraham (John 8:41). But Jesus dropped the ultimate bomb on them when He said, "... *Ye are of* your *father the devil...*" (John 8:44).

***Remember that all of these things were said to people who believed on Jesus* (John 8:30).**

As I said earlier, the thief on the cross was saved by simply believing on the Lord and confessing his faith. You can get to heaven with the minimum requirement of just believing on Jesus. But there are multitudes who think they believe, when the truth is, they are of their father the devil, just as these believers were.

There is a belief that is just an intellectual acknowledgment of truth, and that's not the same as the Bible-believing faith it takes to access true salvation.

James 2:19 says,

Thou believest that there is one God; thou doest well: the devils also believe, and tremble.

If all a person does is acknowledge that God exists, they haven't done anything the devil hasn't done. The devil certainly acknowledges the existence of God. But his whole life is set against God and everything that the Lord loves.

James went on to say,

But wilt thou know, O vain man, that faith without works is dead?

James 2:20

You have to go beyond just acknowledging the truth of God's existence. You've got to do something the devil has never done. You must submit yourself to Jesus as your Lord (Rom. 10:9). That doesn't mean that you commit to never making a mistake or straying from what is right. But you are willing for Jesus to take the lordship of your life. That's the first step in becoming a disciple. There are many other steps to becoming a true disciple, but it starts with turning your life over to the control of Jesus. The devil has never and will never do that.

As I said before, it's difficult to tell if a person has saving faith, but it's not difficult at all to see if a person is a disciple, or on their way to becoming a disciple. If the church was making disciples instead of converts, the world would have a completely different view of Christianity.

Here are some of the things the Lord said about true disciples:

If any man come to me, and hate not his father, and mother, and wife, and children, and brethren, and sisters, yea, and his own life also, he cannot be my disciple. And whosoever doth not bear his cross, and come after me, cannot be my disciple. For which of you, intending to build a tower, sitteth not down first, and counteth the cost, whether he have sufficient to finish it? Lest haply, after he hath laid the foundation, and is not able to finish it, all that behold it begin to mock him, Saying, This man began to build, and was not able to finish. Or what king, going to make war against another king, sitteth not down first, and consulteth whether he be able with ten thousand to meet him that cometh against him with twenty thousand? Or else, while the other is yet a great way off, he sendeth an ambassage, and desireth conditions of peace. So likewise, whosoever he be of you that forsaketh not all that he hath, he cannot be my disciple.

Luke 14:26-33

He that loveth father or mother more than me is not worthy of me: and he that loveth son or daughter more than me is not worthy of me. And he that taketh not his cross, and followeth after me, is not worthy of me.

Matthew 10:37-38

The disciple is not above his *master, nor the servant above his lord. It is enough for the disciple that he be as his master, and the servant as his lord. If they have called the master of the house Beelzebub, how much more* shall they call *them of his household?*

Matthew 10:24-25

A new commandment I give unto you, That ye love one another; as I have loved you, that ye also love one another. By this shall all men *know that ye are my disciples, if ye have love one to another.*

John 13:34-35

Herein is my Father glorified, that ye bear much fruit; so shall ye be my disciples.

John 15:8

Even a surface-level understanding of these scriptures reveals that modern Christianity looks radically different than what Jesus envisioned for His disciples. We have lessened Christianity to something that would be unrecognizable to the first-century Christians. Those early Christians faced persecution that caused many of them to be crucified, burned at the stake, fed to the lions, and rejected in ways that most modern "believers" would never endure today.

The early church didn't have the advantage of radio, TV, books, tracts, the internet, air-conditioned auditoriums, and padded pews. There were no bumper stickers about Jesus being Lord on the camels crossing the desert. But in thirty years, they evangelized the known world. They had a much bigger impact on their world than modern Christianity is having on our world. Why? I believe discipleship is the main reason.

It wasn't popular to be a Christian until the time of Emperor Constantine in the fourth century A.D. Prior to that, you could be put to death for your faith in Christ. This weeded out those who only casually "believed" in Jesus. All that was left were disciples, those who had continued in God's Word until they loved Him more than their own lives (Rev. 12:11).

We need disciples today more than ever. The world has seen the anemic version of Christianity and rejected it en masse. I reject it too. But true Christianity, as displayed in the lives of believers who have become disciples, is the only true hope of humanity.

It is in the darkness that our light shines the brightest. We have a wonderful opportunity to show the world what a true disciple of the Lord Jesus Christ is. We should stand out like a healed thumb in this lost and dying world. We are alive while the world is dead in trespasses and sins. They should be able to tell the difference between life and death.

I heard a story once about a man who died during a church service. The paramedics came and took out half the church members before they found the dead man. That was a dead church! But we are called to life. This life can only be manifested to the world if we continue in God's Word until we become disciples.

The choice is yours. Are you going to be a disciple or just a believer? I beseech you by the mercies of God that you would choose to become a disciple by the renewing of your mind through the Word of God. If you do that, you will prove to yourself and the world that you are a true disciple of the Lord Jesus Christ.

> *I beseech you therefore, brethren, by the mercies of God, that ye present your bodies a living sacrifice, holy, acceptable unto God,* which is *your reasonable service. And be not conformed to this world: but be ye transformed by the renewing of your mind, that ye may prove what* is *that good, and acceptable, and perfect, will of God.*

> Romans 12:1-2

Andrew's teachings are available for free at **awmi.net**, or they can be purchased at **awmi.net/store**.

Go deeper in your relationship with God by browsing all of Andrew's free teachings.

Appendix A

One disciple every six months

After 6 months .... 2 disciples

One year 4

1.5 years 8

2 years 16

2.5 years 32

3 years 64

3.5 years 128

4 years 256

4.5 years 512

5 years 1,024

5.5 years 2,048

6 years 4,096

6.5 years 8,192

7 years 16,384

7.5 years 32,768

8 years 65,536

8.5 years	131,072
9 years	262,144
9.5 years	524,288
10 years	1,048,576
10.5 years	2,097,152
11 years	4,194,304
11.5 years	8,388,608
12 years	16,777,216
12.5 years	33,554,432
13 years	67,108,864
13.5 years	134,217,728
14 years	268,435,456
14.5 years	536,870,912
15 years	1,073,741,824
15.5 years	2,147,483,648
16 years	4,294,967,296
16.5 years	8,589,934,592

End Notes

1. *Online Etymology Dictionary,* "indeed (adv.)," accessed January 28, 2025, https://www.etymonline.com/word/indeed#etymonline_v_6363

2. *Strong's Definitions*, s.v. "μαθητής" ("mathētēs"), accessed January 28, 2025, https://www.blueletterbible.org/lexicon/g3101/kjv/tr/0-1/

3. *Vine's Expository Dictionary of New Testament Words*, s.v., "μαθητής" ("mathētēs"), accessed January 28, 2025, https://www.blueletterbible.org/search/Dictionary/viewTopic.cfm?topic=VT0000751

4. The Kansas City Star. "Why Did Gandhi Say, 'If It Weren't for Christians, I'd Be a Christian?'" Victorville Daily Press, August 26, 2016, accessed January 29, 2025, https://www.vvdailypress.com/story/lifestyle/faith/2016/08/26/why-did-gandhi-say-x2018/985856007/

Receive Jesus as Your Savior

Choosing to receive Jesus Christ as your Lord and Savior is the most important decision you'll ever make!

God's Word promises, *"That if thou shalt confess with thy mouth the Lord Jesus, and shalt believe in thine heart that God hath raised him from the dead, thou shalt be saved. For with the heart man believeth unto righteousness; and with the mouth confession is made unto salvation"* (Rom. 10:9–10). *"For whosoever shall call upon the name of the Lord shall be saved"* (Rom. 10:13). By His grace, God has already done everything to provide salvation. Your part is simply to believe and receive.

Pray out loud: "Jesus, I acknowledge that I've sinned and need to receive what you did for the forgiveness of my sins. I confess that You are my Lord and Savior. I believe in my heart that God raised You from the dead. By faith in Your Word, I receive salvation now. Thank You for saving me."

The very moment you commit your life to Jesus Christ, the truth of His Word instantly comes to pass in your spirit. Now that you're born again, there's a brand-new you!

Please contact us and let us know that you've prayed to receive Jesus as your Savior. We'd like to send you some free materials to help you on your new journey. Call our Helpline: **719-635-1111** (available 24 hours a day, seven days a week) to speak to a staff member who is here to help you understand and grow in your new relationship with the Lord.

Welcome to your new life!

Receive the Holy Spirit

As His child, your loving heavenly Father wants to give you the supernatural power you need to live a new life. *"For every one that asketh receiveth; and he that seeketh findeth; and to him that knocketh it shall be opened...how much more shall* your *heavenly Father give the Holy Spirit to them that ask him?"* (Luke 11:10–13).

All you have to do is ask, believe, and receive! Pray this: "Father, I recognize my need for Your power to live a new life. Please fill me with Your Holy Spirit. By faith, I receive it right now. Thank You for baptizing me. Holy Spirit, You are welcome in my life."

Some syllables from a language you don't recognize will rise up from your heart to your mouth (1 Cor. 14:14). As you speak them out loud by faith, you're releasing God's power from within and building yourself up in the spirit (1 Cor. 14:4). You can do this whenever and wherever you like.

It doesn't really matter whether you felt anything or not when you prayed to receive the Lord and His Spirit. If you believed in your heart that you received, then God's Word promises you did. *"Therefore I say unto you, What things soever ye desire, when ye pray, believe that ye receive* them, *and ye shall have* them" (Mark 11:24). God always honors His Word—believe it!

We would like to rejoice with you, pray with you, and answer any questions to help you understand more fully what has taken place in your life!

Please contact us to let us know that you've prayed to be filled with the Holy Spirit and to request the book *The New You & the Holy Spirit*. This book will explain in more detail about the benefits of being filled with the Holy Spirit and speaking in tongues. Call our Helpline: **719-635-1111** (available 24 hours a day, seven days a week).

Call for Prayer

If you need prayer for any reason, you can call our Helpline, 24 hours a day, seven days a week at **719-635-1111**. A trained prayer minister will answer your call and pray with you.

Every day, we receive testimonies of healings and other miracles from our Helpline, and we are ministering God's nearly-too-good-to-be-true message of the Gospel to more people than ever. So, I encourage you to call today!

About the Author

Andrew Wommack's life was forever changed the moment he encountered the supernatural love of God on March 23, 1968. As a renowned Bible teacher and author, Andrew has made it his mission to change the way the world sees God.

Andrew's vision is to go as far and deep with the Gospel as possible. His message goes far through the *Gospel Truth* television program, which is available to over half the world's population. The message goes deep through discipleship at Charis Bible College, headquartered in Woodland Park, Colorado. Founded in 1994, Charis has campuses across the United States and around the globe.

Andrew also has an extensive library of teaching materials in print, audio, and video. More than 200,000 hours of free teachings can be accessed at **awmi.net**.

Contact Information

Andrew Wommack Ministries, Inc.
PO Box 3333
Colorado Springs, CO 80934-3333
info@awmi.net
awmi.net

Helpline: 719-635-1111 (available 24/7)

Charis Bible College
info@charisbiblecollege.org
844-360-9577
CharisBibleCollege.org

Gospel Truth Network
gtntv.com

For a complete list of all of our offices,
visit **awmi.net/contact-us**.

Connect with us on social media.

Sign up to watch anytime, anywhere, for free.

GOSPEL TRUTH
NETWORK

GTNTV.com

Download our apps available on mobile and TV platforms or stream GTN on Glorystar Satellite Network.

CHARIS
BIBLE COLLEGE

God has more for you.

Are you longing to find your God-given purpose? At Charis Bible College you will establish a firm foundation in the Word of God and receive hands-on ministry experience to **find, follow,** and **fulfill** your purpose.

Scan the QR code for a free Charis teaching!

CharisBibleCollege.org
Admissions@awmcharis.com
(844) 360-9577

Change your life. **Change the world.**

Andrew's LIVING COMMENTARY BIBLE SOFTWARE

Andrew Wommack's *Living Commentary* Bible study software is a user-friendly, downloadable program. It's like reading the Bible with Andrew at your side, sharing his revelation with you verse by verse.

Main features:
- Bible study software with a grace-and-faith perspective
- Over 26,000 notes by Andrew on verses from Genesis through Revelation
- *Matthew Henry's Concise Commentary*
- 12 Bible versions
- 2 concordances: *Englishman's Concordance* and *Strong's Concordance*
- 2 dictionaries: *Collaborative International Dictionary* and *Holman's Dictionary*
- Atlas with biblical maps
- Bible and *Living Commentary* statistics
- Quick navigation, including history of verses
- Robust search capabilities (for the Bible and Andrew's notes)
- "Living" (i.e., constantly updated and expanding)
- Ability to create personal notes

Whether you're new to studying the Bible or a seasoned Bible scholar, you'll gain a deeper revelation of the Word from a grace-and-faith perspective.

Purchase Andrew's *Living Commentary* today at **awmi.net/living**, and grow in the Word with Andrew.

Item code: 8350

ANDREW WOMMACK MINISTRIES